A PLACE IN
HISTORY

THE
BERLIN
WALL

ANNE ROONEY

W
FRANKLIN WATTS
LONDON • SYDNEY

First published in 2010 by Franklin Watts

Copyright © 2010 Arcturus Publishing Limited

Franklin Watts
338 Euston Road
London NW1 3BH

Franklin Watts Australia
Level 17/207 Kent Street, Sydney, NSW 2000

Produced by Arcturus Publishing Limited,
26/27 Bickels Yard, 151–153 Bermondsey Street,
London SE1 3HA

Series concept: Alex Woolf
Editor and picture research: Alex Woolf
Designer: Phipps Design
Map illustrator: Stefan Chabluk

Picture credits:
Arcturus: 11 (Stefan Chabluk).
Corbis: cover *background* (dpa), cover *foreground* (Bettmann), 6–7 (dpa), 8 (Yevgeny
Khaldel), 9 (Hulton-Deutsch Collection), 10 (Bettmann), 13 (Hulton-Deutsch Collection),
14, 15 (Bettmann), 16 (Hulton-Deutsch Collection), 17 (Bettmann), 18 (Bettmann),
19 (Hulton-Deutsch Collection), 20 (Bettmann), 21 (Bettmann), 22 (Hulton-Deutsch
Collection), 23 (Bettmann), 24 (dpa), 25 (Bettmann), 26 (Bettmann), 27 (Bettmann),
28 (Reuters), 29 (Bettmann), 31 (Bettmann), 32 (Bettmann), 33 (Michael Urban/
Reuters), 34 (Christian Simonpietri/Sygma), 35 (Bettmann), 36 (Bettmann),
38 (Bettmann), 39 (Alain Keler/Sygma), 40 (Dieter Klar/dpa), 41 (Dominique Aubert/Sygma),
42 (Gideon Mendel), 43 (Richard Baker).
Getty Images: 12 (Time & Life Pictures), 37 (Keystone/Hulton Archive).
TopFoto: 30 (Topham/AP).

Cover pictures:
Background: A view across the Berlin Wall towards the East, showing Potsdamer Platz.
Foreground: East German policemen carry away the body of 18-year-old Peter Fechter, who
was shot while attempting to escape over the Berlin Wall on 17 September 1962.

A CIP catalogue record for this book is available from the British Library.

Dewey Decimal Classification Number: 943.1'55087

ISBN 978 1 4451 0047 0

Printed in China

Franklin Watts is a division of Hachette Children's Books, an Hachette UK company.
www.hachette.co.uk

SL001439EN

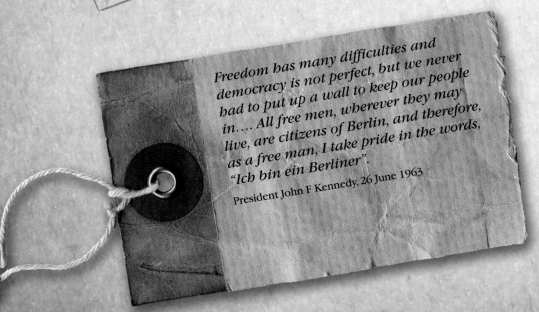
Freedom has many difficulties and democracy is not perfect, but we never had to put up a wall to keep our people in.... All free men, wherever they may live, are citizens of Berlin, and therefore, as a free man, I take pride in the words, "Ich bin ein Berliner".
President John F Kennedy, 26 June 1963.

CONTENTS

1. A CITY TORN IN TWO

The weekend of 12 and 13 August 1961 began like any other summer weekend for the citizens of Berlin. On Saturday 12 August many people visited the countryside, enjoying their free time, some staying out late. But on Sunday morning they awoke to a changed world.

While Berlin slept, the East German authorities split the city in two. Armed guards were stationed along 43 kilometres of barbed wire fencing. They prevented people from crossing between the East and West of the city. Trains, buses, the underground line and roads all stopped at the border. For the next 30 years, the citizens of East Berlin would be kept apart from neighbours, friends and family in West Berlin.

Over the following days and years, the barbed wire became a wall and a strip of empty land, patrolled by armed guards. Anyone trying to cross without permission would be shot. It was a political and physical barrier that tore straight through the heart of Europe.

East German police guard the first barbed wire barrier in Bernauer Strasse, Berlin, on the morning of 13 August 1961.

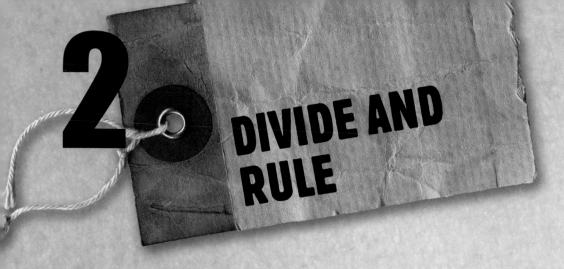

2 DIVIDE AND RULE

Berlin was already a divided and occupied city when the wall went up. It had not been free and self-governing since 1945, when Germany lost World War II.

World War II ended in 1945 with the defeat of Adolf Hitler's Nazi Germany by the Allied powers of the United States, Great Britain, France and the Soviet Union. The Potsdam Agreement of August 1945 fixed the terms of peace, punishing Germany for the war and preventing Germany from rising again to threaten its European neighbours.

The agreement moved back Germany's borders to return land Germany had taken during the war, demanded reparations (compensation) from Germany, and dismantled German industries that could have contributed to a revival of military power. Most importantly, it split the country into eastern and western halves, the East to be administered by the Soviet Union and the West by the Western Allies. The capital, Berlin, lay well within East Germany but it too was to be divided into eastern and western parts.

A Soviet soldier raises the flag of the Soviet Union over the Reichstag in Berlin after the defeat of Germany in 1945.

Refugees who escaped from the Soviet sector of Berlin enjoy a meal of hot soup provided by a relief centre in the British sector.

Uneasy neighbours

Although the communist Soviet Union and capitalist Western powers were forced to work together to fight the Nazis, they deeply mistrusted each other. This would make their joint rule of Berlin both tense and difficult.

In the closing days of World War II, Soviet troops reached Berlin before the Western Allied forces. Soviet troops looted the city and took control, keeping the Western Allies out for as long as possible. When the Western Allies finally entered their part of the city, it was the beginning of an uneasy relationship between the joint occupiers.

The state of the city

Berlin was in a poor state at the end of the war. As Hitler's seat of power, it was heavily

bombed by Allied air forces, while incoming Soviet troops destroyed more on the ground. The population was half what it had been before the war, and 40 per cent of the buildings had been destroyed. There was no power, public transport or working sewer system, and the city could provide only 2 per cent of its food needs. Berlin was also flooded with refugees – up to 12,500 arrived every day in October 1945.

Capitalism and communism

Capitalism and communism are two contrasting political systems. Under communism, wealth and property are controlled by the state, supposedly on behalf of the people. Each citizen works for the common good to the extent of his or her ability, and is provided for by the state in return. In theory, everyone enjoys an equal and adequate standard of living.

A capitalist system promotes private ownership of property. Each person is rewarded according to his or her contribution. As a consequence, some people are rich and others are poorer. However, unlike communist systems, in which the state (government) tends to be very powerful, Western capitalist countries are officially committed to principles of democracy and individual freedom.

The ideal of communism, that society should be equal and no-one should suffer poverty, gained a lot of support in impoverished, post-war Europe. Yet the form of communism that was practised in the Soviet Union fell far short of this ideal. Many people suffered poverty, hardship

British prime minister Winston Churchill, US president Harry Truman and Soviet premier Josef Stalin at Potsdam in August 1945, where the division of Germany and Berlin was negotiated.

and malnutrition. Under the repressive rule of Josef Stalin (1928–1953), the Soviet state employed a very large network of police and informers to keep control of the population. Millions of innocent people were sent to harsh prison camps.

VOICES

Soviet arrival in Berlin

Berlin … [was] completely under control of the Red Army. The last days of savage house-to-house fighting and street battles had been a human slaughter, with no prisoners being taken on either side. These final days were hell…. We were a city in ruins; almost no house remained intact.

Dorothea von Schwanenfluegel, Berlin resident in 1945

10

Berlin divided

Under the Potsdam Agreement, Berlin was divided into three sectors, managed by the United States, Britain and the Soviet Union. The French were later granted their own sector, carved out of the British portion.

At first, the division of Germany, and Berlin, was seen as a temporary measure, until a new government could be established in Germany that was satisfactory to all the occupying powers. But as relations deteriorated between the Soviet Union and the Western Allies, cooperation between the two sides broke down and the division of both the country and the city became more entrenched.

Although Berlin was 160 kilometres inside East Germany, the Western Allies were determined to maintain their presence there, partly because it allowed them to keep watch on what was happening in Eastern Europe. For the same reason, the Soviet Union disliked the Western presence in Berlin.

FACT FILE

Sport returns to Berlin

Berlin hosted the Olympic Games in 1936, and Hitler turned it into a great propaganda victory for his Nazi regime. Hitler later used the Olympic stadium for some of his grand Nazi rallies. In 1946 British troops reopened the closed stadium for an eight-nation field-and-track event for the Allied forces stationed in Berlin.

Berlin was divided between Allied and Soviet occupiers, mirroring the division of Germany as a whole.

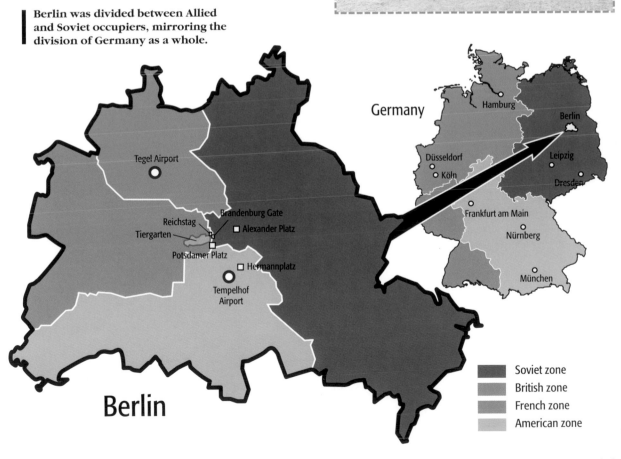

Germany

Hamburg
Berlin
Düsseldorf
Köln
Leipzig
Dresden
Frankfurt am Main
Nürnberg
München

Tegel Airport
Brandenburg Gate
Reichstag
Tiergarten
Alexander Platz
Potsdamer Platz
Hermannplatz
Tempelhof Airport

Berlin

- Soviet zone
- British zone
- French zone
- American zone

3. THE COLD WAR CHILL

Suspicion between East and West in the post-war period soon turned to open hostility. This was partly because of the sharp contrast between the ideals of communism and capitalism. Also, both sides feared and distrusted the intentions of the other. The tension between them became known as the Cold War, the defining conflict of the second half of the 20th century. It was never an open war, but a dangerous stand-off between two world superpowers, the United States and the Soviet Union, together with their allies.

Eastern Europe goes communist

By the end of World War II, the Soviet army controlled the whole of Eastern Europe, including eastern Germany, Poland, Czechoslovakia, Hungary, Bulgaria, Romania and Yugoslavia. At first, Western leaders agreed with this arrangement, seeing it as a temporary measure until elections could be held and democratic governments elected.

However, Stalin had no intention of losing control of Eastern Europe. The Soviet Union had lost around 20 million of its people in World War II – more than any other country – and Stalin believed that a 'buffer zone' of

British prime minister Winston Churchill gives the speech at Fulton, Missouri, on 5 March 1946, in which he introduced the phrase 'iron curtain'.

VOICES

The Iron Curtain

From Stettin in the Baltic to Trieste in the Adriatic an iron curtain has descended across the Continent. Behind that line lie all the capitals of the ancient states of Central and Eastern Europe.... all these famous cities and the populations around them lie in what I must call the Soviet sphere, and all are subject ... not only to Soviet influence but to a very high and ... increasing measure of control from Moscow.

British Prime Minister Winston Churchill, speaking at Fulton, Missouri, USA, 1946

Citizens of divided Berlin were able to make some contact with each other through the barbed wire fence, which was the first barrier. The wall soon prevented such close contact.

friendly nations was necessary to protect the Soviet Union from future aggression.

Soon, all the countries of Eastern Europe had permanent communist governments friendly to the Soviet Union. This happened by a process of elections, intimidation and the gradual removal of opposition. Only Yugoslavia was later able to become independent of the Soviet Union. Many in the West feared that the communist takeover of Eastern Europe was merely the first stage in a planned conquest of Western Europe. The invisible line dividing communist Eastern Europe from democratic Western Europe became known as the Iron Curtain, a phrase taken from a speech given by Winston Churchill in 1946 (see panel).

FACT FILE

The Warsaw Pact

As the world divided into East and West, military alliances followed. In 1949 the United States, Canada and ten Western European nations formed the North Atlantic Treaty Organization – NATO. According to its first Secretary General, NATO's purpose was 'to keep the Russians out, the Americans in, and the Germans down'. If any NATO member was attacked, it would be treated as an attack on the whole alliance and the whole alliance would retaliate. In 1955 the Soviet Union formed a similar military alliance of Eastern Bloc countries (communist states of Eastern Europe) known as the Warsaw Pact.

A demonstration against the Marshall Plan in East Berlin. The Soviets distrusted the Marshall Plan, viewing it as an attempt by the United States to swing Europe away from communism.

The Marshall Plan

After a very cold winter in 1946–1947, much of Europe was starving and nearly bankrupt. France and Italy appeared to be on the brink of turning to communism. The US Secretary of State General George Marshall proposed an aid plan to help Europe and discourage any temptation to support communism. The Marshall Plan, as it became known, began in 1947. Marshall claimed it was 'directed not against any country or doctrine, but against hunger, poverty, desperation, and chaos'. Aid was also offered to Eastern Europe, but Stalin refused it, seeing it as a ploy to undermine Soviet control.

Indirect wars

Hostility between the United States and the Soviet Union increased from the late 1940s and throughout the 1950s. The Cold War spread to almost every continent as each side tried to promote its cause in conflicts around the globe. The Soviet Union generally supported communist or national liberation movements fighting to overthrow European colonial rule. The United States supported any regimes it felt were under threat from communism, even if they were undemocratic or oppressive.

FACT FILE

The Chinese Civil War

In China, during the civil war between the Communist Party, led by Mao Tsetung, and the ruling Kuomintang, the United States supported the Kuomintang and the Soviet Union supported the communists. In 1949, Mao's forces won and China became a communist state. Indirect wars such as this became a feature of the Cold War. The superpowers avoided direct confrontation, fearing it might escalate into a nuclear war.

The arms race

At the start of the Cold War the only country with nuclear weapons was the United States. The power of these weapons was demonstrated when the United States dropped two atom bombs on Japan at the end of World War II, each one destroying a city. The Soviet Union was determined to acquire its own atom bomb and achieved its aim in 1949. In 1952 the United States developed a hydrogen bomb, hundreds of times more powerful than the atom bomb. Both sides rushed to stockpile and test ever more powerful nuclear weapons and missile systems to deliver them. An arms race began.

Soon both sides had enough nuclear weapons to destroy the world many times over. A nuclear war would have brought the end for humankind. This situation was aptly known as MAD – Mutually Assured Destruction. The fear of such a catastrophe probably prevented the Cold War ever escalating into a 'hot' war.

VOICES

MADness

After a full nuclear exchange such as the Soviet bloc and the NATO alliance are now able to carry out, the fatalities might well exceed 150 million. The devastation would be complete and victory a meaningless term.

US Defense Secretary Robert McNamara, 1962

The characteristic 'mushroom cloud' produced by detonating a nuclear bomb became an icon of the fear that gripped the world during the Cold War.

4 CRISIS IN BERLIN

The state of the economy in both West and East Germany was dire after World War II. The burden of paying reparations crippled Germany, particularly in the East, where the Soviets dismantled German factories and railways and took them back to the Soviet Union.

Trizonia

Britain and the United States realized that the economic destruction of Germany would

West German currency was worth much more than East German currency. Men trading currency on the black market at Bahnhof Zoo could expect 20 East German marks for one West German mark.

not benefit them in the long run and decided on a series of measures to help. One of these was to form 'Bizonia' in 1947, a trade alliance of the parts of West Germany controlled by the United States and the UK. When the French added their own zone to the alliance, it became 'Trizonia'. The establishment of Trizonia further alienated the Sovet-occupied sector from the Western sectors. It was the first step towards the formal separation of Germany into two nations.

By this time, the German currency, the Reichsmark, had become so devalued that cigarettes were being used as currency instead. On 18 June 1948, the United States and the UK replaced the devalued Reichsmark in Bizonia with the new

Bundesmark, revitalizing the economy overnight. When the Western Allies extended the new currency to West Berlin, the Soviet Union responded with fury.

The blockade and airlift

This added to the Soviet Union's determination to expel the Western Allies from Berlin. In the spring of 1948 the Soviet Union withdrew from the Allied Control Commission that jointly governed Germany. Then, from midnight on 24 June 1948, the Soviets closed all land routes into West Berlin, cutting off supplies of food, fuel and raw materials.

Determined not to abandon the people of West Berlin, the UK and United States launched a daring and ambitious plan to supply the Western sectors by air. A continuous stream of aeroplanes delivered supplies to the West Berliners.

The Soviet Union, realizing they could not win, finally ended the blockade on 12 May 1949. The Western Allies continued sending in supplies until 30 September in order to build up stockpiles in case of another siege.

Besieged West Berliners watch as an American plane arrives to deliver food and other essential supplies during the Berlin airlift in 1948.

CT FILE

The airlift in numbers

- By October 1948, 147,581 tonnes of supplies were coming into West Berlin each month on 600 planes a day.
- In April 1949, 7,845 tonnes were landed in a single day; by Easter a plane landed almost every minute.
- 17,000 volunteers helped to build a new airport at Tegel from ten million bricks salvaged from the war-damaged city. It was ready for the airlift to use on 5 November 1948.

The pilots who brought the supplies became heroes to the people of Berlin. They boosted their popularity even further by dropping luxuries such as sweets so that the planes became known as *Rosinenbomber* (Raisin Bombers).

Two Germanies

In 1949 East and West Germany officially became independent countries – the Federal Republic of Germany in the West and the German Democratic Republic (GDR) in the East. West Berlin remained as an outpost of West Germany deep inside East Germany. It was not going to be an easy position to occupy.

After Stalin

Stalin was a ruthless dictator. Under his rule, millions of people died in the gulag (prison or labour camps) or starved as a result of his disastrous economic and agricultural policies. During Stalin's life, any resistance to his authority or criticism of his policies was met with immediate, brutal punishment.

After he died in 1953, the Soviet Union began a process of 'de-Stalinization' under the new leader Nikita Khrushchev. Although not the tyrant Stalin had been, Khrushchev was still a strict communist. He was aggressive and prone to angry outbursts. Khrushchev was in almost constant conflict with Walter Ulbricht, the leader of East Germany and a supporter of Stalin.

FACT FILE

Death in the gulag

The gulag was a network of brutal prison camps in Siberia. It was started in 1919 and built up by Stalin, who filled it with political opponents and suspected anti-communists. Around 12 million people died in the gulag, from over-work, cold, starvation and brutality at the hands of guards and other inmates. The gulag was largely dismantled by Khrushchev in the mid-1950s.

Demonstrators from East Berlin march through the Brandenburg Gate into the Western sector after the violent rioting of the Berlin Uprising in 1953.

Soviet tanks appear on the streets of Budapest in 1956 as the Hungarian uprising is ruthlessly crushed. Around 3,000 Hungarians were killed in the fighting and some 20,000 fled the country.

Attempts at revolt

People in the Eastern Bloc were dissatisfied with the low standard of living and their repressive, Soviet-backed governments. However, any attempts at reform or rebellion were quickly crushed. In East Germany, a government decision to put up taxes and prices and increase work quotas without increasing wages led to a strike and protests in June 1953. The uprising was put down quickly and violently by forces from East Germany and the Soviet Union.

In 1956 a student demonstration in Budapest, Hungary, quickly grew into a full-scale revolution that overthrew the communist government. The new government planned to withdraw Hungary from the Warsaw Pact and declared itself independent from the Soviet Union. Soviet tanks and troops crushed the revolution in November 1956 and reinstated a communist government.

VOICES

Hungarian uprising

More tanks and troops are pouring in than were present at the height of the German occupation in World War II. The Soviets' negotiation of withdrawal turns out to be a cruel ruse, typical of their tactics throughout the Cold War. Column after column of troops, tanks and heavy artillery is entering the city from the east and are securing all the vital centers. The largest cannons are being erected on Gellérthegy (Gellert Hill) and are now pounding the entire city. The shelling is so fierce in our neighborhood that we must leave our apartment and hunker down in the bomb shelter beneath our building.

Peter Stricker, Budapest resident, private account, November 1956

19

5. BUILDING THE WALL

While West Germany prospered, thanks to the Marshall Plan and the new currency, East Germany fell further and further into poverty. Many East Germans dreamed of a new life in the West. Berlin became a particular focus of discontent – and the scene of many escapes. Stopping the flow of people out of the East became a major preoccupation for East German and Soviet leaders.

Exodus from Berlin

As the 1950s progressed, conditions in East Germany worsened. Food supplies dwindled and more property was confiscated and taken into state ownership. Despite Soviet propaganda, East Germans could see that West Germans enjoyed a better standard of living.

Hungry East Berliners make a dash for food hand-outs in West Berlin in 1953. Soviet authorities banned East Berliners from taking the food, and people had to brave security guards to get it.

FACT FILE

The flow from East to West

From 1955 around a quarter of a million people left East Germany each year, many crossing from East to West Berlin. The number dropped slightly in 1959, then rose dramatically in 1960, with 20,000 leaving in May alone. In total, over 2.6 million people fled East Germany between 1949 and 1961.

Increasing numbers fled to the West, including many professionals (such as doctors, teachers and engineers) leaving a labour and skills shortage in East Germany.

The East German leader Walter Ulbricht was desperate to stem the flood. He had persuaded Stalin in 1953 that a formal barrier was needed between East and West Berlin. Stalin agreed to this, but died soon afterwards, and when Khrushchev took over he shelved the plan. He knew a wall would be controversial and wanted to delay any drastic action until he had met the new US president, John F Kennedy, in Vienna in June 1961.

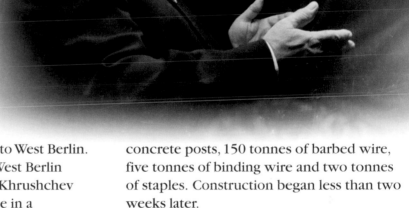

US president John F Kennedy and Soviet premier Nikita Khrushchev talk outside the Soviet embassy in Vienna after an unproductive meeting in 1961.

Leaders meet

The meeting between Khrushchev and Kennedy was ill-tempered and unproductive. Khrushchev threatened to close all access to West Berlin. Kennedy pledged to protect West Berlin from Soviet aggression while Khrushchev threatened to wipe out Europe in a thermonuclear war and make sure Kennedy was 'the last president of the United States'.

Secret plans

The first hint that Ulbricht planned a wall came at a press conference on 15 June 1961. He denied any plans to build a wall – but no-one had suggested there was such a plan. On 6 July Khrushchev gave the go-ahead for the wall, and Ulbricht put his secretary for security matters Erich Honecker in charge of the project. Only senior members of the government knew what was happening.

On 1 August the border police began to collect the required supplies: 18,200 concrete posts, 150 tonnes of barbed wire, five tonnes of binding wire and two tonnes of staples. Construction began less than two weeks later.

VOICES

Thinking the unthinkable

There was heated debates among friends and workmates, and everyone sensed that something dramatic was going to happen. But a wall right through the city, as was occasionally suggested? No, our imaginations didn't stretch that far.

Joachim Trenkner, East Berlin resident

The barricades go up

At midnight on 12 August 1961 Honecker gave the command to start erecting the barricade. A total of 10,000 security police, 7,000 soldiers, 240 tanks and 320 armoured personnel carriers moved into position. Together they sealed off all checkpoints and blocked all roads, underground lines and train lines crossing into West Berlin. They then began to raise a barbed wire barrier all around the Western sectors of the city. Underground, sewage and service tunnels were stopped at the border. The Brandenburg Gate, the symbolic centre of Berlin that stood on the dividing line between East and West, was sealed. Mail and telephone links between East and West were cut. West Berliners woke up to find themselves isolated from the outside world.

West Berliners trapped on the wrong side of the barrier were allowed home as long as they could show papers to prove they lived in the West, but East Berliners could no longer cross into the West for work or to visit friends and relatives. Two days later, workers began to replace parts of the makeshift barrier with the beginnings of a wall built from concrete blocks and brick.

From wire to wall

Within the next few months the barrier was rebuilt – as a wall topped with barbed wire in some places and an improved wire fence in others. The wall was just over 1.5 metres high. From June 1962 parts of the barrier were replaced with an improved wall, and a second fence was built 100 metres further inside East Berlin. Buildings between the two barriers were destroyed, and this no-man's land, which came to be known as the death strip, was patrolled by soldiers instructed to shoot to kill.

A new wall was started in 1965, made of concrete slabs and posts and steel girders, topped with a concrete sewage pipe to make it difficult to climb. In 1975 the wall was replaced for the last time, with a barrier built of 45,000 pre-fabricated concrete panels, again topped with a tube. The new wall was 3.6 metres high (excluding the tube).

Responses to the wall

The shock and anguish of Berliners at the division of their city carried little weight outside Germany. The West was unwilling to provoke the Soviets at a tense time in the Cold War. Since the wall was in East Berlin, to restrict East Germans, West Berlin was not threatened and so the Western Allies could get away with doing nothing. Willy Brandt, the mayor of West Berlin and later Chancellor of West Germany, was furious.

Soviet tanks and soldiers patrol a checkpoint on the Berlin Wall in February 1961.

An East German construction worker helps build the Berlin Wall near the Brandenburg Gate.

FACT FILE

An anti-fascist protective rampart

The East German government justified the wall as a means of protecting their citizens. It claimed that the West had been kidnapping, poaching and corrupting East Germans. They called the wall an *antifaschistischer Schutzwall* – an anti-fascist protective rampart.

How the wall worked

By 1989 the wall was a double barrier encircling West Berlin. Raked gravel in the death strip showed up footprints easily, revealing the tracks of escapees and showing whether border guards were patrolling properly. The death strip was overlooked by watch towers, illuminated by floodlights and protected by electric fences, dogs, minefields and trenches to stop vehicles. People who were allowed to cross between West and East had to go through special checkpoints. The most famous was Checkpoint Charlie at Friedrichstrasse, used by NATO personnel, diplomats and foreign tourists to enter East Berlin.

Tank barriers at Potsdamer Platz in East Berlin in August 1962. This deserted square was one of the busiest parts of Berlin before the building of the wall.

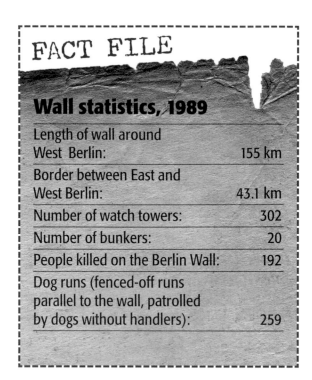

FACT FILE

Wall statistics, 1989

Length of wall around West Berlin:	155 km
Border between East and West Berlin:	43.1 km
Number of watch towers:	302
Number of bunkers:	20
People killed on the Berlin Wall:	192
Dog runs (fenced-off runs parallel to the wall, patrolled by dogs without handlers):	259

Stand-off at the wall

For a few days after the barrier appeared, only West Berliners objected. But soon the United States gave its support to West Berlin, stationing additional troops in the city. In October a stand-off between US and Soviet troops at Checkpoint Charlie seemed likely to start a conflict. Border guards demanded to examine documents before allowing a US diplomat to cross into East Berlin, though diplomats did not officially have to show them. The argument escalated and soon tanks were lined up ready to fire. The matter was resolved peacefully, but the episode demonstrated how delicate the situation in Berlin had become.

In 1963 US president Kennedy visited West Berlin. The speech he made within sight of the Brandenburg Gate marked a key moment in East–West relations. He spoke in support of West and East Berliners, condemning the Soviet system and pledging support for the divided city (see panel).

What the West really thought

Although Western governments complained in public that the wall was an outrage against the people of Berlin, they privately welcomed it for two main reasons. Firstly, it represented a significant propaganda victory, showing Western citizens that the Soviet regime was closed and despotic, relying on a physical barrier to keep hold of its people. Secondly, the wall reduced political tension within Berlin, making it far less likely that the East would invade West Berlin. By entrenching the division of the city, the wall had paradoxically made West Berlin safer.

US president John F Kennedy looks at the Berlin Wall from his speaking platform on 26 June 1963. A short time later, he made his famous 'Ich Bin Ein Berliner' speech.

VOICES

Ich bin ein Berliner

There are many people in the world who really don't understand ... the great issue between the free world and the communist world. Let them come to Berlin. There are some who say that communism is the wave of the future. Let them come to Berlin.... Freedom has many difficulties and democracy is not perfect, but we never had to put up a wall to keep our people in.... All free men, wherever they may live, are citizens of Berlin, and therefore, as a free man, I take pride in the words, "Ich bin ein Berliner".

President John F Kennedy, 26 June 1963

6. LIFE IN THE EAST AND WEST

In the early days after the wall went up, Berliners had to adjust to living in a divided city. Over the following 30 years, the lives of people in the East and West would diverge, developing separately, though just metres apart.

Wall of shame

The wall divided friends and families. It was known by many Berliners as the *Schandmauer*, or 'wall of shame'. It also separated some 60,000 people, called 'border crossers', from their work. These people lived in the East but worked in the West and were generally unpopular in East Berlin. The currency in West Berlin was worth more than the currency in East Berlin, so border crossers were much richer than their fellow East Berliners.

While NATO personnel could cross to East Berlin at approved checkpoints, Berlin citizens could not cross at all, except for occasional arrangements at Christmas (see panel), until 1971. After that date, West Berliners could apply for a visa to allow visits to East Berlin. Most East Berliners, however, could only visit West Berlin in very exceptional circumstances.

Lifestyles in the East and West

In West Berlin, like the rest of Europe, the 1960s were a time of economic prosperity.

A woman stands on a stepladder in Bernauer Strasse in West Berlin and waves to friends or family in East Berlin. In the early days, before the wall became very high, this was a common way for people in the divided city to keep in touch.

FACT FILE

Christmas visits, 1963

In 1963, a new word entered the German language: *Passierscheinregelung*. It was the name for the special arrangement that allowed West Berliners to visit East Berlin over the Christmas period that year. The visits were allowed again in 1964, 1965 and 1966.

Food and consumer goods were in plentiful supply, and West Berliners were free to buy whatever they could afford, including televisions, refrigerators, fashionable clothes and exotic foreign foods.

In East Berlin, people had less money and less choice. They could only buy things produced in the Eastern Bloc, which tended to be ugly, utilitarian and of poor quality. Under East Germany's centrally planned economy, the state established production targets and fixed wages and prices. This system tended to be very inefficient, and there were often shortages of basic goods including food, fuel and clothes.

East and West Berliners greet each other at the Oberbaum Bridge border crossing point, open for Christmas visits for the first time in 1963.

VOICES

On duty in Berlin

Driving through Checkpoint Charlie was like driving off the set of a colour movie and into film noir. The sky was grey. The buildings were grey. The clothes were grey. The people were grey. They shuffled along, slumped over, looking very tired. Mostly people ignored us, but some walked by and without turning their heads, winked or raised an eyebrow to say hello – knowing full well that if they got caught they would be arrested and possibly never seen again.

S Agliano, 8th Infantry, Germany, 1969–1972

State-run media

The East Germans had not chosen the communist system but had it forced upon them. Their resentment increased the more they saw of the prosperity in the West. The government-controlled media in East Germany tried to hide this from them and ignore or deny the harsh economic and social conditions in the East. Most East Berliners, though, listened to a radio station called RIAS, broadcast by the United States from West Berlin, and were keenly aware that their lives were much poorer and harder than those of their neighbours.

Under the eye of the Stasi

Many East Berliners were keen to escape to West Berlin. The wall served to prevent this, but in addition a ruthless and efficient secret police force, the Stasi, worked to spy on and keep track of East Berliners.

The Stasi obtained much of its information from ordinary citizens informing them about their neighbours' activities. This created a climate of fear and suspicion – anyone could be an informer. The Stasi kept detailed records of the most trivial details of people's everyday lives. If they visited a friend, the Stasi would record when they went, where they went and even what they ate there, if they could find out.

VOICES

Shaming defectors

Is it not despicable when for the sake of a few alluring job offers or other false promises about a 'guaranteed future' one leaves a country in which the seed for a new and more beautiful life is sprouting, and is already showing the first fruits, for the place that favors a new war and destruction?

Agitator's Notebook, published by the Socialist Unity Party's Agitation Department, Berlin District, November 1955

Some of the millions of files on East German citizens held at the Stasi headquarters in Berlin. The files, which would stretch for 112 kilometres if laid out flat, were opened to the public in 1992.

Watching the enemy

Berlin stood very much on the front line of the conflict between the two superpowers and was sometimes called 'the capital of the Cold War'. Unsurprisingly it was filled with spies. The West spied on the East, and the East spied on the West. They used a battery of tricks and techniques, including bugs, secret cameras, hidden tunnels, sleepers, moles, double agents, concealed weapons, fake documents and all the paraphernalia of espionage familiar from spy novels and films. In addition to trying to discover military and political secrets, spies from the West helped East Germans defect (escape) to the West.

FACT FILE

Günter Guillaume

Escaping to the West as a defector provided a way for some East German spies to infiltrate Western security forces, intelligence services and governments. Günter Guillaume 'fled' to the West in 1956 as a refugee, but in fact continued to work for the Stasi. He was trusted in West Germany and became the personal assistant of Willy Brandt (then chancellor) in 1972. In 1974 Guillaume was uncovered and arrested. Brandt resigned, ending his political career.

The Glienicke (or 'Unity') Bridge was sometimes used for the exchange of captured spies between East and West Berlin.

YOU ARE LEAVING
THE AMERICAN SECTOR
ВЫ ВЫЕЗЖАЕТЕ ИЗ
АМЕРИКАНСКОГО СЕКТОРА
VOUS SORTEZ
DU SECTEUR AMÉRICAIN
SIE VERLASSEN DEN AMERIKANISCHEN SEKTOR

7. OVER (AND UNDER) THE WALL

Many people desperate to escape from East Berlin took great risks to do so. Soviet guards followed a shoot-to-kill policy. The death strip was laced with trip-wires and mines, and the fence on the eastern side of the death strip was electrified. Around 200 people died while attempting to escape, but many succeeded and began a new life in the West.

> Nineteen-year-old East German soldier Conrad Schumann jumps the barbed wire barrier on 15 August 1961. His family had already fled to the West.

The first days

As soon as the first barrier went up, some people made immediate attempts to escape from East Berlin. While there was just a simple barbed wire barrier it was not too difficult to get across. One of the most famous escapees was a young East German border guard, Conrad Schumann, who was manning the new barricade. Encouraged by Western onlookers and police, Schumann jumped the wire. The famous photo of his leap became a symbol of the flight to freedom.

VOICES

Manning the wall

We felt we were simply doing our duty but were getting scolded from all sides. The West Berliners yelled at us and the Eastern demonstrators yelled at us. We stood in the middle…. For a young person, it was terrible.

Conrad Schumann, border guard who escaped to West Berlin, 15 August 1961

Other escapes were more traumatic. The border ran down Bernauer Strasse, so that a house could be in the East but face the road in the West. Many people jumped from windows on 13 August while East German police tried to stop them. Some died in the attempt.

The Soviets soon tightened security along the border, making escape considerably harder. Yet over the next 28 years around 10,000 people tried to defect, of whom about 5,000 succeeded.

Over the wall

In the early days of the wall, when the barrier was relatively low, many people tried to go over it. The simplest way was to jump, as Schumann had done, or to use rope – but the sale of rope was soon restricted in the East. Later, there were more ambitious escapes. Two men shot an arrow attached to a cable over the wall to a roof in West Berlin, then attached pulleys to the cable and sailed across the wall.

Two families created a home-made hot-air balloon from small pieces of nylon fabric and sailed over the wall. Following the escape, the sale of thin fabric was restricted in East Berlin. A group of young mechanics made a chain of folding ladders guided by pulleys and ropes and used it to cross an electrified section of wall without touching it.

Hundreds of East and West Berliners watched helplessly as Peter Fechter bled to death at the foot of the wall after being shot by East German guards while trying to escape. He was the 50th person to die at the wall.

FACT FILE

Peter Fechter

On 17 August 1962 an 18-year-old bricklayer, Peter Fechter, was shot trying to escape. He bled to death in no-man's land; Soviet forces did not allow anyone to help him. He became a symbol of the wall's victims, and wreaths and memorials marked the spot where Fechter fell.

FACT FILE

Radio over the wall

In the Eastern Bloc the media were controlled by the Soviet state authorities. News was censored and filtered, keeping the population ignorant of anything negative about life in the East. Often, the 'news' was propaganda and lies; information about the West was distorted or withheld. More accurate news was broadcast in German by RIAS (Rundfunk im amerikanischen Sektor – Broadcasting in the American Sector), a station set up by the United States. Many East Berliners depended upon it as a source of uncensored news, cultural programmes and commentary. At times, 80 per cent of the Berlin population listened to RIAS.

Under the wall

Over the years a large number of tunnels appeared beneath the city, many of them dug by college students. This was easier in the first years of the wall. Once the death strip was added, tunnels had to be considerably longer.

The first known successful tunnel began in a graveyard. People would take flowers, pretend to mourn, and then disappear into the tunnel, coming out in West Berlin. Another began in the basement of a house at 60 Westerstrasse and was used by 29 people. In the early years, service tunnels and sewers also provided ready-made routes, but these were soon policed. Over 100 people escaped through one sewer that the East German authorities forgot to seal.

Through the wall

People tried to go through the wall by force or deception. One truck full of East Berliners simply crashed through the wall. At a blind spot between two checkpoints, several people swam a small river to escape. British soldiers provided a rope ladder on the Western side of the river to help the swimmers climb out.

Many people were smuggled through checkpoints using false papers or were hidden in cars. Often people were crushed into hidden compartments of cars, or even suitcases. Sometimes they had to stay there for hours, in constant fear of being discovered and then killed.

Helping hands

Friends in West Berlin and NATO personnel often helped people escape. One young woman made a fake US army uniform, begging buttons and badges from army officers by saying she wanted them for a play. Wearing her uniform, she took a US car into the East and brought back two friends.

Official help was not just an act of kindness but helped to undermine Soviet authority and embarrass East Berlin. The Western Allies would help individuals to escape and give them transport to a place where they could start a new life in the West. Defectors were even given money and practical assistance.

Klaus Jacobi (right) and Manfred Koster stand behind a specially adapted BMW Isetta. Jacobi made a secret compartment in which he smuggled Koster to West Berlin in 1963. Eight people escaped in modified Isettas.

VOICES

Helping them out

It was ugly, horrible. It was like living in a prison. These East Berliners would come up and beg us, 'Take us to West Berlin'. The amount of people I personally brought over my government never knew. I would have been relieved of my duty.... It was a joyous time for us to help people be free.

Verner N Pike, US serviceman stationed in Berlin, from a TV interview recorded in 2006, talking about his memories of 1961

33

8. THE COLD WAR CONTINUES

Although most closely watched in Berlin, the Cold War was played out on the world stage. As with China in 1946–1949, the superpowers continued to support opposing sides in conflicts around the globe rather than fighting each other directly.

US soldiers of the 1st Division of Airborne Infantry on duty in South Vietnam in 1966 during the Vietnam War.

FACT FILE

The Soviet invasion of Afghanistan

In 1979 the Soviet Union sent 100,000 troops into Afghanistan to support the tottering communist regime there. The United States funded the Muslim mujahedeen to fight against the communists until the Soviet Union withdrew in 1989.

Battles in Asia and Africa

In the Korean War (1950–1953) the United States supported South Korea against invasion from communist-ruled North Korea. China and the Soviet Union supported the North Koreans. Around four million lives were lost in the three-year conflict, but the superpowers stopped short of open confrontation.

During the civil war in the African nation of Angola in 1975, the United States provided weapons for the anti-communist forces, while Cuba – communist since 1959 – sent troops to fight alongside the communists.

In the Vietnam War (1964–1973), US troops actively supported South Vietnam against Viet Cong communist rebels, who were supported by communist North Vietnam. US military power proved ineffective in this case and by 1975 all of Vietnam and neighbouring Cambodia and Laos had communist governments. This was a severe setback for the United States, as it extended the influence of the Soviet Union and China.

The Cuban Missile Crisis

The most perilous moment in the Cold War came when the United States discovered, in October 1962, that the Soviet Union was installing nuclear missiles in Cuba, a Caribbean island just 144 kilometres from the US coast. During two weeks of tense negotiations, the world came very close to a catastrophic nuclear war. Finally, on 28 October, the Soviet Union agreed to dismantle the missiles. The Cuban Missile Crisis has been called the most dangerous point in human history.

Although the crisis ended peacefully, it had a significant legacy. The Soviet authorities lost confidence in Khrushchev, who they felt had caved in too easily to pressure from Kennedy. The Soviet leader was removed from power two years later. Also, a telephone hotline was set up between Moscow and Washington to allow immediate communication between the leaders of the superpowers. Delays of up to 12 hours in receiving and decoding messages from Moscow had increased the global threat during the crisis, and the hotline was designed to avoid such a danger in future.

A Soviet cargo ship carries supplies to Cuba, where the Soviet Union was installing nuclear missiles aimed at the United States during the Cuban Missile Crisis of 1962.

VOICES

Crisis in Cuba

I found myself in the difficult position of having to decide on a course of action which would answer the American threat but which would also avoid war. Any fool can start a war, and once he's done so, even the wisest of men are helpless to stop it – especially if it's a nuclear war.

Nikita Khrushchev, quoted in *Khrushchev Remembers*, Little Brown, 1970

The Cold War in space

During the 1950s and 1960s the Soviet Union and the United States competed with each other in a 'space race'. The Soviet Union won the early victories, being the first to launch a rocket and then a man into space. In 1961 President Kennedy announced the US goal of putting a man on the moon before the end of the decade. Huge resources were devoted to the project, which was successfully achieved in 1969.

The space race was not just a matter of national pride and propaganda – the United States feared that a presence in space might give the Soviets a military advantage. The idea of space as a Cold War battleground was revived in 1983 when US president Ronald Reagan announced the development of a 'Star Wars' weapon system that would be capable of intercepting Soviet missiles from space. The system never appeared, but caused alarm and panic in Moscow.

The rocket that blasted Soviet cosmonaut Yuri Gagarin in the Vostok spaceship into space in 1961, on display in 1967 at the Exhibition of Economic Achievement in Moscow.

FACT FILE

Space race timeline

- **4 October 1957:** The Soviet satellite Sputnik 1 is the first artificial object in space.
- **3 November 1957:** Sputnik II carries the dog Laika, the first living creature launched into space.
- **12 April 1961:** Soviet cosmonaut Yuri Gagarin is the first man in space.
- **20 July 1969:** US astronaut Neil Armstrong is the first man on the moon.

Science secrets

After World War II, senior Nazi scientists were secretly welcomed into the United States and the Soviet Union, where they helped with weapons development and the rocketry that eventually led to space exploration.

The United States continued to recruit enemy scientists during the Cold War, this time from the Eastern Bloc. Spies and defectors revealed the extent of Soviet weapons development, or offered their expertise for the benefit of the United States. Similarly, the nuclear secrets of the West leaked out through Soviet spies in the United States.

Klaus Fuchs fled to Britain from Nazi Germany in 1933. He was a communist and feared for his safety in Germany. As a physicist he was welcomed in Britain and the United States and worked on the Manhattan Project to build the first atom bomb. In fact he was spying for the Soviet Union and passed Western nuclear secrets to the Soviets for 14 years. Security forces in Britain failed to detect his activities.

Physicist and spy Dr Klaus Fuchs (left) meeting his nephew at an airport in East Berlin in 1959. Fuchs moved to East Germany after serving nine and a half years in a British prison for supplying nuclear secrets to the Soviet Union.

VOICES

Deceived by a Soviet spy

The British security service, MI5, knew that Fuchs had communist sympathies, yet they failed to spot that he was a spy and cleared him to work on the Manhattan Project.

[Klaus Fuchs] is rather safer in America. It would not be easy for Fuchs to make contacts with communists there…. It would not appear desirable to mention his proclivities to the authorities in the United States.

Major Garrett, MI5, 1944

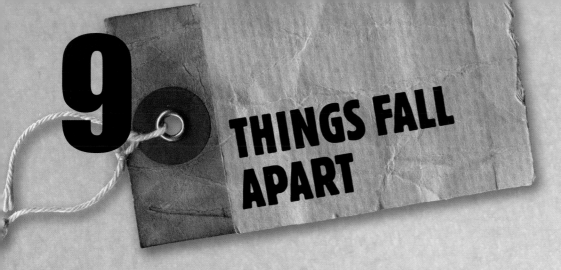

9. THINGS FALL APART

In 1983 Ronald Reagan denounced the Soviet Union as an 'evil empire'. Both sides were as hostile as ever and the Cold War looked set to continue into the foreseeable future. But in reality the Soviet Union was starting to crumble. Its centrally planned economy was woefully inefficient and unable to meet the needs of its population or its requirements as a military superpower.

A young Czech girl shouts at Soviet soldiers sitting on tanks in the streets of Prague during the 'Prague Spring' uprising in 1968.

Golden years

The Soviet regime was at its strongest in the 1970s. It overtook the United States in the number of nuclear weapons it had, and the Soviet Union's territorial hold over Eastern Europe was internationally recognized with the Helsinki Final Act of 1975.

In 1972 Soviet leader Leonid Brezhnev began talks with US president Richard Nixon to limit nuclear arms, beginning an era of 'détente' when the tensions of the Cold War lessened. But it was not to last. By the 1980s

the Cold War had chilled again and the Soviet Union was in a bad state. Enormous spending on arms and the space race, as well as a failing agricultural policy, left the Soviet Union nearly bankrupt and struggling to feed its huge population.

Signs of revolt in Europe

The first hint of rebellion in the satellite states came in Czechoslovakia in 1968. The new leader Alexander Dubcek attempted to introduce a wide range of reforms, giving people greater freedom. A few months later the Soviets sent a Warsaw Pact army to invade Czechoslovakia. Dubcek was removed and a more hardline communist leader was installed.

In 1980 shipworkers in Poland formed a new trade union called Solidarity, led by Lech Walesa. Solidarity demanded better conditions. It was banned and martial law was imposed in Poland.

Communism on the wane

In 1985 a new, reformist leader, Mikhail Gorbachev, took power in the Soviet Union. His policies of Perestroika (restructuring) and Glasnost (openness) introduced some elements of free enterprise and political transparency. Central control of the economy was loosened and privately owned businesses were encouraged. Also, people were allowed to comment on government policies and discuss political ideas other than communism. However, Gorbachev's economic reforms were ineffective, and by giving people more freedom he merely hastened the end of the Soviet era.

> # VOICES
> ## *Soviet planes over Prague*
> *I'd been woken up by the sound of the aircraft overhead…. It was a very scary sight – this dark night, and all these planes without lights, like huge dark crosses flying over our heads…. I can remember the sense of desperation I felt…. I felt my future had been lost.*
>
> Ondrej Neff, a journalist for Czechoslovak Radio in 1968, recalling the Soviet invasion during a 2008 interview

Polish union leader Lech Walesa is carried on the shoulders of fellow shipyard workers as they celebrate the official founding of the independent trade union Solidarity.

Berlin stands firm

Conditions improved somewhat in East Germany. Ulbricht was replaced by Erich Honecker in 1971. Honecker adopted a policy of 'consumer socialism', which allowed East Berliners some of the comforts of the West and gave them the highest standard of living in the Eastern Bloc. But Honecker was not soft. He hoped to deter citizens from defecting to the West, yet he planned for the wall to last 100 years.

The view from the West

Many Western nations were pleased to see the curtain coming down on the communist era. US president Ronald Reagan – who had always taken a strong anti-communist line – visited Berlin in 1987. Standing in front of the wall, he called for the East to pull it down (see panel). However, UK prime minister Margaret Thatcher harboured a secret wish that the wall would remain, as a unified Germany could threaten Europe again.

Opening borders

As the Soviet Union became more open, the other Eastern Bloc countries followed suit. In 1988 Gorbachev announced that they were free to decide their own policies – the Soviet Union was no longer going to intervene in their internal affairs. In 1989 Hungary opened its borders with the West. Soviet troops and tanks did not arrive in force as they had in 1956, but defectors from other parts of Eastern Europe did.

When Hungary opened its borders, more than 13,000 East Germans took the opportunity to flee to the West through Budapest. Many had visas, but others left illegally. In the summer and autumn of 1989, 25,000 East Germans escaped through the West German embassy in Prague.

VOICES

Reagan in Berlin

There is one sign the Soviets can make that would be unmistakable, that would advance dramatically the cause of freedom and peace. General Secretary Gorbachev, if you seek peace, if you seek prosperity for the Soviet Union and Eastern Europe, if you seek liberalization: Come here to this gate! Mr. Gorbachev, open this gate! Mr. Gorbachev, tear down this wall!

President Ronald Reagan, Berlin, 12 June 1987

US president Ronald Reagan delivers a speech at the Berlin Wall in front of the Brandenburg Gate in June 1987.

On 10 November 1989, Berliners from East and West celebrate by climbing on top of the wall that had divided their city for 28 years.

The fall of the wall

Protests across East Germany led to the resignation of Honecker in October, and of the communist government in November. A crowd of a million people gathered for a pro-democracy rally in the main square in East Berlin. Then, at midnight on 9 November 1989, the authorities gave permission for the checkpoints at the wall to be opened. After 28 years, the wall fell quickly and peacefully. People were at last allowed to cross from East to West Berlin without hindrance. Jubilant East Berliners flooded through the gates, and soon people were clambering onto the wall and hacking it down. West Germans welcomed people from the East with flowers and parties.

FACT FILE

Honecker's plan backfires

Honecker hoped to shame the East German defectors. Those who were granted exit visas were put in sealed trains that travelled through East Germany and Czechoslovakia into Hungary. However, people lined the route to cheer the trains and throw flowers. It was hardly the effect Honecker had hoped for.

A new life

As East Germans arrived in West Germany, many immediately destroyed the symbols of their old lives in the East. Some ripped up East German money or abandoned their ugly, old-fashioned East German cars in the streets. West Germany welcomed them with help to start a new life, including money and assistance in finding jobs.

After the collapse of the East German regime, angry East Germans ransacked the offices of the Stasi and scattered or destroyed the secret files documenting the lives of their fellow citizens.

FACT FILE

End of the Stasi

As the wall fell, the offices of the Stasi were filled with faithful employees shredding the documents they had so carefully compiled since 1945. The shredded documents are now being pieced together using special computer software. It's a big task – there were around 16,000 bags of documents. Anyone is now able to look at their Stasi files – and everyone who lived in or even visited East Berlin had a Stasi file.

Those who stayed in the East also looked forward to a new way of life, though following a slower process of change.

After the wall

On 3 October 1990 Germany was reunified. After the initial euphoria, there followed a difficult period for former East Germans. Those who moved to the west found it hard to integrate, and 20 years on, the east of Germany had still not caught up with the prosperity of the west. Some West Germans resented the influx of East Germans who needed money and jobs and who seemed to many to be taking a lot but giving little back. East Germans themselves, traumatized by decades of being watched by the Stasi, often found it hard to cope with freedom. Germans still talk of the 'wall in the head', which defines the difference between East and West Germans. For the people of Berlin, only the youngest have no memories of the wall and of the division of their city. It will take a long time for the wounds of the division to heal.

End of the Cold War

The government of Czechoslovakia was overthrown peacefully in the so-called Velvet Revolution in November 1989, but other regimes ended more violently. There was bloodshed in Romania and a three-and-a-half year civil war in the Balkan states. However, by the end of 1990, communism had collapsed in Eastern Europe and the Cold War was over. The Soviet Union disbanded itself at the end of 1991. Russia has abandoned communism, and China has opened itself to a market economy, leaving only North Korea, Laos, North Vietnam and Cuba as old-style communist powers. Today, the threats to world peace lie elsewhere. We no longer live in fear of conflict between the communist East and capitalist West, and Berlin is now a peaceful and united city.

VOICES

Gone but not forgotten

It's still present in a lot of heads and I don't think that's going to change in our generation. My cousin was pro-Western, but she grew up and went to school in a different system. But the next generation – her daughters and her grandchildren – that's where it's more or less disappeared.

Elke Kielberg, aged 12 in 1961, a resident of Bernauer Strasse, West Berlin, interviewed for a German TV programme in 2006

Six months after the fall of the Berlin Wall, a former resident of East Berlin glances over her shoulder, perhaps nostalgically, at an abandoned Trabant car in eastern Berlin.

GLOSSARY

atom bomb A nuclear weapon that derives its energy from nuclear fission – the splitting of atoms.

capitalism An economic system based on the private ownership of wealth, characterized by a free market and motivated by profit.

censor Restrict what someone can say or show.

colonial Relating to colonies, or territories which have been taken over by and ruled as satellites of another state.

communism A system, or the belief in a system, in which capitalism is overthrown and the state controls wealth and property.

cosmonaut A Soviet astronaut.

defection Leaving a country for political reasons to live somewhere with a different political system.

détente Relaxing or easing of a tense political situation.

double agent A spy who pretends to work for one side while actually working for the enemy.

Eastern Bloc Countries in Eastern Europe allied with or controlled by the Soviet Union.

entrenched Fixed and likely to remain for a long time.

espionage Spying activity.

euphoria Extreme happiness.

fascism A nationalistic, often racist, ideology that favours strong leadership and does not tolerate dissent.

gulag The collection of harsh prison work camps in Siberia, north-east Russia.

hydrogen bomb A nuclear weapon that derives some of its energy from nuclear fusion – forcing the nuclei of atoms to fuse together.

infiltrate Establish a presence within enemy territory without the enemy's knowledge.

informer Someone who passes on information about others to security services or enemies.

integrate Become an accepted member of a group.

intercept Prevent an object from reaching its destination by stopping, diverting, seizing or destroying it.

Iron Curtain A term used to describe the border between East and West in Europe during the Cold War.

MAD Mutually Assured Destruction – the situation in which two powers possess such extensive weaponry that if one destroys the other, their own destruction is also automatically assured.

martial law A situation in which civil government and civil law enforcement are suspended and the military imposes law and order.

mole A spy who has taken a job in the security services or another sensitive area and passes secret information to an enemy state or rival.

Nazi A member of the German National Socialist party, a fascist party led by Adolf Hitler, which ran Germany from 1933 to 1945.

nuclear weapon A weapon that derives its explosive force from the energy within atoms.

occupied Ruled by another power, which has invaded and has an army in place to keep order.

paraphernalia Equipment.

propaganda Organized publicity, often by a government, to promote a particular view.

quota An allocated amount.

refugee A person who flees from persecution or hardship in his or her own land.

reparations Compensation demanded of a defeated state by the victor after a war.

repressive Exerting strict control on the freedom of others.

sleeper A spy who remains inactive in an organization for a long time but at some point passes sensitive information to a rival.

Stasi The East German secret police service.

thermonuclear weapon A weapon that takes at least some of its energy from nuclear fusion.

trip-wire A wire connected to a bomb or mine that is detonated when the wire is moved.

visa A permit to enter a country.

FURTHER INFORMATION

BOOKS

Days That Changed the World: The Fall Of The Berlin Wall: November 9th, 1989 by Jeremy Smith (TickTock Media, 2004)

Snapshots in History: The Berlin Wall: Barrier to Freedom by Michael Burgan (Compass Point Books, 2007)

Turning Points in History: The Fall of the Berlin Wall by Nigel Kelly (Heinemann, 2007)

When the Wall Came Down: The Berlin Wall and the Fall of Communism by Serge Schmemann (Kingfisher Books, 2006)

The Who's Who of the Cold War by Clive Gifford (Wayland, 2009)

WEBSITES

www.berlin.de/mauer/index.en.html
A comprehensive site about the wall and its history.

www.die-berliner-mauer.de/en/45.html
An illustrated timeline of the division of Berlin and the Berlin Wall, 1945–89.

www.nytimes.com/interactive/2009/11/09/world/europe/20091109-berlinwallthennow.html
Before-and-after photos of the wall.

VIDEOS

Berlin Wall – Escape To Freedom (DVD) Pegasus Entertainment, 2008

www.youtube.com/watch?v=eSwmBacyIP4&NR=1
Archive footage from CNN and the BBC of the building of the wall.

www.youtube.com/watch?v=HEbsCYLx2TI&feature=related
News footage of the fall of the wall (in German with English subtitles).

www.youtube.com/watch?v=LdZVsFjWnbI
Scenes from the construction and destruction of the wall.

INDEX

Page numbers in **bold** refer to pictures.